C000015576

OTHER HELEN EXLEY GIFTBOOKS

To a very special Dad   For a Beautiful Daughter

A Little Book for a Friend   To my very special Wife

The Love between Fathers and Daughters

SELECTED BY HELEN EXLEY
ILLUSTRATED BY JULIETTE CLARKE

Published simultaneously in 2003 by Exley Publications Ltd in Great Britain,
and Exley Publications LLC in the USA.

Copyright © Helen Exley 2003. The moral right of the author has been asserted.

12 11 10 9 8 7 6 5 4 3 2 1

ISBN 1-86187-302-6

A copy of the CIP data is available from the British Library. All rights reserved.
No part of this publication may be reproduced in any form. Printed in China.

**Exley Publications Ltd, 16 Chalk Hill, Watford, Herts WD19 4BG, UK.
Exley Publications LLC, 185 Main Street, Spencer MA 01562, USA.
www.helenexleygiftbooks.com**

Acknowledgements: The publishers are grateful for permission to reproduce
copyright material. Whilst every reasonable effort has been made to trace copyright
holders, the publishers would be pleased to hear from any not here acknowledged.
Pam Brown, Aurelia Cholet, Banou Corbeau, Natasha Clarkson,
Pamela Dugdale, Sylvie Dupont, Charlotte Gray, Stuart and Linda Macfarlane,
Sian E. Morgan, Helen Thomson, Pascal Umbert, Jenny de Vries:
published with permission © Helen Exley 2003.

A LITTLE BOOK FOR MY
Dad

A HELEN EXLEY GIFTBOOK

Your dad is there
to add sparkle
and surprise
to your childhood.

SIÂN E. MORGAN, B.1973

A LOVE THAT'S SO STRONG

He loves his children
not only because everything in
them is lovely and according to
his liking, but because there is a
real incomprehensible bond
which is stronger than fiction.

LEROY BROWNLOW,
FROM "A FATHER'S WORLD"

Romance fails us
and so do friendships,
but the relationship
of parent and child,
remains indelible and
indestructible,
the strongest relationship
on earth.

THEODOR REIK (1888-1969)

Dad's love...
Warm on a winter's day,
Gentle when times are hard,
Funny when I feel down,
Firm when I'm being ghastly,
...everything I ever need.

LINDA MACFARLANE, B.1953

Any man can become a father.
It takes love to become a dad.

PAM BROWN, B.1928

*When a little child
pulls at his jacket and demands
a lion to play with,
the most solemn dad
goes down on hands and knees
and roars.*

CHARLOTTE GRAY, B.1937

Who rode me on his shoulders,
high and safe and all-seeing,
above the crush of crowds?
Who lifted me to touch the oak
tree branches, to make discoveries
beyond enclosing walls, to watch
the bright processions pass?
Who scooped me up and let me
share his vision? My dad.

JENNY DE VRIES

MAGICAL WALKS

When I was little, my father
used to take me on magical
walks. He would point out
the beauty all around us, a leaf,
a stone – everything that he
touched and explained to me
seemed to come alive and be
magical.

ARKIE WHITELEY

A GENTLE MAN

He was a kind, gentle man,
my refuge whenever anything
went wrong.
He made me feel
that I was very special.

ESTHER PETERSON

What children are looking for is a hug, a lap, a kind word, a touch, someone to read them a story, somebody to smile and share with.

JOHN THOMPSON

My dad is the backbone
of our family.
Any problem that I've ever had,
he's always been there for me.

WHITNEY HOUSTON, B.1963

LIFE DOESN'T COME WITH
AN INSTRUCTION BOOK —
THAT'S WHY WE HAVE FATHERS.

H. JACKSON BROWN

If I were asked to name the world's greatest need, I should say unhesitatingly; wise mothers and... exemplary fathers.

DAVID O. MCKAY

THERE IS NOTHING SO SAFE AS A FATHER'S ARMS.

PAM BROWN, B.1928

Every day of my life has been
a gift from him... His arms
have sheltered me from teenage
heartbreak. His wisdom and
understanding have sustained me
as an adult.

NELLIE PIKE RANDALL

A dad is the one man you count on never betraying you.

SIÂN E. MORGAN, B.1973

A dad's children give him the courage to accept the utter trust they place in him.

PAMELA DUGDALE

Nothing is more important
to children — regardless of their age,
six or thirty-six — than a father
who keeps his word.

CAMPBELL ARMSTRONG,
FROM "ALL THAT REALLY MATTERS"

Dads don't care if you've got an enormous spot, you wear thick glasses, forget your lines in the school play, come last in the races or don't get promoted at work… they're there to love you anyway.

SIÂN E. MORGAN, B.1973

3/10
lazy
effort.

DADS HAVE FAITH
IN YOU, EVEN WHEN
YOU DON'T.

PASCAL UMBERT

Dads take their children's hands and lead them into the wider world — showing them the things they have loved — trees and moors and rivers, castles and museums. And the children return his gifts a thousand-fold — showing him the things that he had long forgotten. Dew-hung spider webs, puddles, the march of rain.

PAM BROWN, B.1928

Daddy; a soft heart.

RENEE

Dads often hover in the background like guardian angels ready to come to your aid in any way they can.

SIÂN E. MORGAN, B.1973

How can one say no to a child? How can one be anything but a slave to one's own flesh and blood?

HENRY MILLER (1891-1980)

Of course I had no idea
I could feel so deeply,
or that tucking children
in would have the serenity
of prayer, or that being
their father would renovate
my heart.

HUGH O'NEILL,
FROM "A MAN CALLED DADDY"

JUST AN ORDINARY GUY

You take a guy, an average guy,
someone with nothing outstanding
going for him... And there by his
side is his kid. All this kid wants is
this guy's eye; his hand; a look;
a hint... The guy touches the kid,
rubs its head, takes its hand,
and the kid looks at him as if
this is heaven.

MARK GREENSIDE

SO PROUD OF ME!

IT WAS EASY TO FIND
MY DAD IN THE HUGE
CROWD AT MY GRADUATION
CEREMONY…
HE WAS THE ONE
WITH THE BIGGEST GRIN.

SIÂN E. MORGAN, B.1973

Even when you're last in the egg
and spoon race a dad sees
the grace in your style.

STUART AND LINDA MACFARLANE

*A father is a fellow who has
replaced the currency in his wallet
with snapshots of his kids.*

MIKE FOREST

A DAD IS BORN

A dad only fully realises his new
responsibilities when his baby
enfolds him in its absolute trust.

. . .

The new father takes up the baby's tiny hand, enfolds it in his own — and the child begins to learn its contours, its weight, its texture, the scent of its skin that will throughout its young life mean security and love.

PAMELA DUGDALE

LOVE AT FIRST SIGHT

*All priorities in a man's life
shift as this little head snuggles
into his shoulder.*

CHARLOTTE GRAY, B.1937

How good to see this erstwhile
rather solemn young man
bending to kiss his baby as he passes,
scooping it up into a cuddle,
showing it flowers and cats
and paper windmills.
And he is overwhelmed by joy —
for the baby's face lights up
when he comes into view.
And reaches out its arms.

PAM BROWN, B.1928

I Need Him

...my dad is my hero. I'm never
free of a problem nor do I truly
experience a joy until we share it.
I need him to know when
I'm hurting. I need him to know
when I'm happy. I need him
to know to hear me....

NANCY SINATRA, B.1940

There's something about a dad that makes you less afraid of the dark, recover more quickly after a shock, make spiders less scary, cuts hurt less and cruel words from other people less upsetting.

SIÂN E. MORGAN, B.1973

It's a wonderful feeling when your father becomes not a god but a man to you — when he comes down from the mountain and you see he's this man with weaknesses. And you love him as this whole being, not as a figurehead.

ROBIN WILLIAMS, B.1952

Dads are there to pull you out of the water if you start to sink… but they're also there to step back a little each time so that you have to push yourself that little bit further.

SIÂN E. MORGAN, B.1973

Dads don't just give their children love they give them the ability to love.

STUART AND LINDA MACFARLANE

The minute he walked in the door at night, even the house seemed to take on a new energy, like a surge of electricity. Everything became charged, brighter, more colorful, more exciting....

VICTORIA SECUNDA

Dads take the business
of building sandcastles very
seriously, it has to be
a masterpiece big enough
to live in and it has to be
the best one on the beach.

PASCAL UMBERT

THE TROUBLE WITH DADS

*The trouble with dads is they
like to dangle you upside down
until you think you're going to
bang your head on the floor.
And they sometimes forget you
get bigger every day and
occasionally you do bang your
head on the floor!*

SIÂN E. MORGAN, B.1973

Mothers bathe their little
children. Dads create tidal
waves and terrible typhoons,
attack with yellow ducks and
loofah submarines.
Saturate towels and flood
the floor. And mothers sigh –
but smile to see such jubilation.

PAM BROWN, B.1928

A Big Kid!

In every real man a child is hidden who wants to play.

FRIEDRICH NIETZSCHE
(1844-1900)

*When toy guides
say 'from three years
upwards',
the 'upwards' bit
is referring
to your dad.*

SIÂN E. MORGAN, B.1973

Poor Dad!

Fathers know their place –
last in the line for the shower
and first in the line
to pay for everything.

STUART AND LINDA MACFARLANE

Sometimes when he gets mad at me I can understand why.

MICHELLE WAGNER

THE THINGS HE'LL DO FOR YOU

A dad is the only person who will get up at 3am to put your gift together, ready for when you wake up. He'll take you to the beach and eat sandwiches with sand in them, just because you made them. And he's the only person who'll sit on a little chair with his legs up to his chin to play a game.

SIÂN E. MORGAN, B.1973

If a man smiles at home
somebody is sure to ask him
for money.

WILLIAM FEATHER

A father is burdened by the fact
that none of his children believe
he has no secret source of wealth.

PAM BROWN, B.1928

Hand out the weekly allowances twice a week. Never say "No". Give freely — your time, your money, your car... your sanity.

STUART AND LINDA MACFARLANE

HOW EMBARRASSING!

There's an unwritten rule that says all dads must tell terrible jokes. And this usually happens most when you're with people you wish you weren't.

SIÂN E. MORGAN, B.1973

You have to love your dad very much when he comes last in the Father's Race for the third year running.

PAM BROWN, B.1928

To cap it all he can't even understand his computer. How embarrassing!

HELEN THOMSON, B.1943

Parents are the bones
on which children sharpen
their teeth.

PETER USTINOV, B.1921

Reasoning with a child is
fine, if you can reach the
child's reason without
destroying your own.

JOHN MASON BROWN

Children are a great comfort
in your old age. And they
help you reach it sooner too.

LIONEL M. KAUFFMAN

People think that children
are messy... they ought to take
a look at some dads!

SYLVIE DUPONT, B.1945

Dads have a habit of making
a mess and forgetting to put
things back where they were.
Then they try and blame it on
you or the dog!

SIÂN E. MORGAN, B.1973

LAZY DADS!

I don't think dads realize that we know they're just pretending to be asleep if we want them to do something... we can see them peeking out of the corner of their eye!

BANOU CORBEAU (1946-1997)

The quickest way for a parent to get a child's attention is to sit down and look comfortable.

LANE OLINGHOUSE

Just when you think your dad
wants to play with you, you realize
it's your toys he's after!

AURELIA CHOLET

*You soon come to realize that dads
have to test out your toys before they
give them to you and that sometimes
this process takes a very long time,
including after you've gone to bed!*

NATASHA CLARKSON

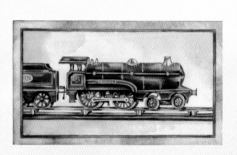

HE SPOILS YOU ROTTEN!

A father is for being talked into being a butterfly in my school play.

ROBIN ROSENBALM, AGE 11

I always remember my dad taking us to the cinema... it wasn't until much later I found out he hated the cinema... but he took us because we loved it.

SIÂN E. MORGAN, B.1973

*The way to a dad's pocket
is through his heart.*

STUART AND LINDA MACFARLANE

*If I wanted something from my father,
I would put my little feet together
pigeon-toe style, tilt my head, and smile.
I got what I wanted every time.*

SHIRLEY MACLAINE, B.1934

Everyone needs a dad
to turn to when things
get rough. Just to be there.
Just to bring back the
feeling of being utterly,
completely safe.

PAM BROWN, B.1928

My guide, my companion, my mentor, my supporter, my defender, but always most of all my closest and surest friend... We would sometimes squabble over trivialities, but always knowing in our hearts that nothing could ever change how we felt about each other and, in my case, that here was the rock I could always turn to.

JACK NICKLAUS, B.1940

NOTHING BUT SUMMER, SUMMER

Ever since she could remember he had been everything in life to her... They had done everything together, shared everything together, dodged the winters together, settled in charming places, seen the same beautiful things, read the same books, talked, laughed, had friends...

*All the years were years of
sunshine. There had been no
winters; nothing but summer,
summer and sweet scents...
He was the most amusing
companion to her, the most
generous friend, the most
illuminating guide, the most
adoring father....*

ELIZABETH VON ARNIM (1866-1941)

All round the world
dads walk, slow stepping,
with their children's tiny hand
clasped safely in their own.
For a little while at peace,
out of the buffeting of
poverty and war.

PAM BROWN, B.1928

Words have an awesome impact. The impressions made by a father's voice can set in motion an entire trend of life.

GORDON MACDONALD

The words that a father speaks to his children in the privacy of home are not heard by the world, but, as in whispering-galleries, they are clearly heard at the end and by posterity.

JEAN PAUL RICHTER (1763-1825)

A dad is not remembered by his children as he is by other people. They treasure small things, silly things —
the texture of his hands,
the shape of his fingernails —
the balding patch on the top

of his head – the crinkles
round his eyes – his bony feet
– all precious.

PAM BROWN, B.1928

WHY, IF WE SAY
WE DON'T REALLY
NEED HIS APPROVAL,
DO WE KEEP
WISHING FOR
IT ALL OUR LIVES?

SIÂN E. MORGAN, B.1973

He loved me and longed for me
before I was born,
Taught me to love books and ride
my bike,
Took my photograph on my first day
at school,
Nursed me when I was ill,
Never criticized my taste in music
or fashion,
Put up with my noisy efforts to be

a drummer in a rock band,
Comforted me when I failed
my exams,
Sang at my wedding,
My dearest hope is that one day my
kids will have such memories of me.

STUART MACFARLANE, B.1953

You'd been my guide, Oubaas Father.
My initiator. My elephant. My deepest
yesterdays had been coloured by you.
When I was very small — do you
remember? — and we walked home at
night, you carried me on your
shoulders. Your shoulders were a ship.
I felt your rough cheeks under my
palms, I could reach up and pluck
the swinging stars.

BREYTEN BREYTENBACH, B.1939
FROM "RETURN TO PARADISE"

SAFETY AND SECURITY

Dads are our silent pillars
of strength, often standing
in the shadows, working
their magic, so much so,
that we can sometimes
forget that they are there.

SIÂN E. MORGAN, B.1973

My father held a cherished place in my life. He encouraged me continually... He gave me the safety, the security, and the consistency to fly as high as my wings would take me.

HENRIETTA DAVIS BLACKMON

What is a Helen Exley Giftbook?

Helen Exley Giftbooks cover the most powerful of all human relationships: the bonds within families and between friends, and the theme of personal values. No expense is spared in making sure that each book is as thoughtful and meaningful a gift as it is possible to create: good to give, good to receive. You have the result in your hands. If you have loved it – tell others! There is no power on earth like the word-of-mouth recommendation of friends.

For a full list of Helen Exley's books, write to:
Helen Exley Giftbooks
at 16 Chalk Hill, Watford, WD19 4BG, UK,
or 185 Main Street, Spencer, MA 01562, USA,
or visit
www.helenexleygiftbooks.com